JEALOUSY AND OTHER TERMS OF ENDEARMENT

"LOVE" POEMS

By Cliff Turner

Jealousy and Other Terms of Endearment

ISBN   978-1-312-80333-6 (Print)
ISBN   978-1-312-80332-9 (E-book)

A grand, romantic gesture
The silver screen, melty kind
It all spiralled down from there
But it's OK, he doesn't mind

An excerpt from a long-discarded poem.

Contents

Longing

Halfway

Her eyes hold me here.
On this cursed, wooden vessel,
plagued with rats and thieves.
It's been two weeks now.
My fear compounds
with each creak of the boards.
Every wave a disaster,
at least, in my mind.
I've twice been robbed
and once beaten.
Not being a man of the sea, I've
become entertainment
for those who are at home here.
Even the rats seem to laugh
as I flounder,
out of my element.
My stomach turning.
My feet stumbling.
My mind lurching.
The waves, the rats, the people;
all gnawing at me.
Even as I've trusted my life to them.
But she is on the other shore,
and we are halfway.
And so,
her eyes hold me here.

Power Lines

It is the sky I am supposed to be in awe of.
Purple, salmon, and rose clouds,
a canvas for the last moments of the sun.
… But …
It is the power lines between those and me that I see.
They grip my mind with suggestions of connection.
How far do they reach?
Across counties? Across borders?
Across possibilities? Across dreams?
If I followed them, accepting my instinct at each
intersection,
allowing my inner beast to guide me along their
spiderweb path,
would they bring me to my goddess?
That sky above, you see, it is the colour of me,
when I am in full release, entwined with another,
for that brief moment exiting the physical as my seed is
extracted.
That is the colour that my spirit becomes, the colour of
that glorious sky.
The purple, salmon, and rose palette above those wires is
me.
Could those suspended lines take me to the one whose
colours would swirl with mine?
Many nymphs and fairies have tried.

But, alas, the physical is the only place they've joined me.

My goddess exists, I know this!

The one whose spirit would dance in the heavens with mine.

Our bodies sweaty below,

our essence glowing above.

And now the wires beneath the glorious sky become my hope.

The purple beast within me growls.

Aching, it tells me to go,

follow, search, and explore.

The goddess awaits.

Dream 1813

I awoke from a dream
in which I awoke
from a dream

    the deeper of the two
    1813, separated by the sea
    searching for you
        only letters and anecdotes
        but to no avail
        only hopes you'd seen my notes

        awaken to the other dream
        two foxes out the window
        I sip whisky as they trot toward me
    in a cabin with you
    did I find you in 1813
    and why are you see-through

I awoke from a dream
in which I awoke
from a dream

Shopping Cart
(a micro story)

She pondered their ignorance to her problem and its precious solution, which she'd cleverly hidden deep within her shopping cart. As she pushed it across the street, she could feel their eyes avoiding her. Averted by the guilt-fuelled, spiritual nausea people like her seemed to induce. The dirty sleeping bag, the sack of empty bottles, the random scraps of tarp and cardboard were a shield from their concern.

They could not see what put her there. The loss of a daughter and a husband. The anguish and descent from that terrible moment. The desperate efforts and gut wrenching deeds made necessary to survive since then.

Only a day ago, as with the past four years, she would have petitioned for their sympathy. She would have endured their judgements and looks of disgust as she asked for spare change, for a tiny push toward survival. Today, though, she slipped quietly by them. Eyes down, singing softly while gently easing her cart over the curbs.

She could barely hear the screaming as it echoed from the park a block away. The panicked cry of a young mother finding her baby carriage empty.

Vacancy

"What else could nails be for?"
She wondered
Alone
In a nameless hotel
Six floors above the lounge
Her only use for them?
To hold love in
Downstairs she'd had her choice
Sipping her drink
Hunting
Calculated seduction
They all watched her
They all pined for her
They all lusted for her
She chose a dark-haired one
He looked like he once was handsome
A salesman
Compressors or tools or something
In his drunken lostness
In his lost loneliness
In his lonely drunkenness
He'd said he loved her
After he was spent

But now she finds herself alone
Again
Barely three hours later
So the nails became useful
To hold that love in
For all it's worth

The Trickster

"I am the true trickster."
       Said time
       His eyes gleaming with delight
"This realm is no one's but mine."

"Let me show you…"
       And with a wave of his hand
       A picture formed from nothing
"…how I control this land."

"See these two?"
       The figures walked as in a cloud
       Side by side and hand in hand
"I've picked them from among a crowd."

"To toy with at my will."
       He moved to look upon the scene
       With a smile and somehow a frown
"If I'd have just let things be, you see, …"

"…this picture would be true."
       He breathed and then the fog was gone
       Erasing the two as if they had never been.
"But I crossed their paths too soon."

"She needed her angels."
　　　He painted a new picture to see
　　　One that he meddled in
"He needed to find how to be."

"Neither could provide the other's need."
　　　He wrapped his hands tightly
　　　Basking in his devious glee
"So that's when I linked their souls, you see."

"Haha! Now what can they do?"
　　　He laughed at his plots
　　　So proud of himself, he said
"They rule each other's thoughts."

"Yet because of me they can only wonder …"
　　　His voice dropping just a tad
　　　His tricks now seen clearly
"… what joy they could have had"

"Unless some day I decide,"
　　　He said with a smirk and some glee
　　　The thought of it making him giggle
"Unless some day I let them see."

Eavesdropping on Romance

A brunette and a blonde
On a patio sipping coffee
Tight pants
Sunglasses
Comparing last night's dates

Some guy named Joshua
Unemployed
Not studying
Took the brunette to a music festival
Danced a lot (tee hee)
Not going to see him again

The other was Timothy
Works a lot (yawn)
Focused
Talks too much
Picked the blonde up for dinner
In a cool car
Not going to see him again

I wonder what Josh and Tim
Are saying about
The brunette and the blonde

Romance?

His need for love
was far greater
than his knowledge
of love's mechanics.
Creepy
Annoying
Clingy
He'd heard them all
but couldn't understand.
Disney couldn't be wrong …
Right?
Isn't this romance?
Trying to be
where she is …
Just to talk
Just to be seen
Just to be noticed
… by her.
He couldn't understand
why.
Why?
Why did her man
step in?
Why did she allow it?
Doesn't she see love?
Romance?

After Date 23

… or was it #28?

All the right swipes
                turned out to be wrong.
        What if a left swipe
                would have been right?

Alone tonight.
                It's too late.

Graveyard Kiss

Their tongues entwine
Among the ghosts
Their passions as cold
As the graves below

For now it's fine
But they both know
It's simply hope
To not be alone

Among the shrines
Their lies unfold
But nothing grows
All truth be told

They so resign
Their hopes for more
The night ends forlorn
At her bedroom door

Shedding Petals

"He loves me."
"He loves me not."
Two petals from each flower

Moving fast
Between each stem
With each she's less empowered

Lonely days
New men by night
Each one goes home without her

She is one
Who craves one more
Less hope with each encounter

"He loves me."
"He loves me not."
Two petals from each flower

The Danger of Listening Well

He's heard this before …

"Would it be alright
To tug at your shirt sleeve?
To cry on your shoulder?
To expel my pain?
No, it's not attraction
I simply need to talk
And maybe some advice
Would it be alright?
I'll tell you all I feel
About his lack
About my struggle
About my newfound needs
But no, it's not attraction
I simply need to talk
And maybe some advice
Do you think I'm right?
Do you think I'm justified?
Do you think I'm pretty?
I'm glad to have a friend like you
It's certainly not attraction
I simply need to talk
And maybe some advice
You've listened all night

Why isn't he like you?
Thank you for caring
Will you hold me?
No, it's not attraction
I simply need to talk
And maybe some advice, but,
Maybe more would be nice."

Hurting

Clean Sheets

Her bed
Our bed?
No ... her bed
Though I lie in it nightly
I am a stranger here
Unwelcome
She has made it so
Through an invitation to another
Accepted
Her territory has been marked
She might as well have pissed on it
So here I lie
In metaphorical piss
Counting the money I'll lose
When I leave

Body Pillow

How is that four-foot-long pillow?
Your replacement for your replacement of me.
Was he, like I, unaware of your slow switch?
As you bitchily played both our hearts,
Begging for love and care,
While you withheld your own.
Ego driven games of greed and lust.
Shattered trust!
And where are you now?
With a four-foot-long pillow.
Dead feathers. No heart. No embrace.
The stink of your desire melted to it,
After many lonely and lustful nights.
Better that pillow than me.

She Died Yesterday

She died yesterday
A heart problem
The physical kind
   shovelled onto the metaphorical
We shared one night
   years ago   Buried
in non-chronological memory
Valueless
   hollow, coffin-like intimacy
Empty sex
The kind reserved for the lonely
   the desperate
     the dead
A feeble attempt
   to cling briefly to humanity
Now she clings no more
   and I am numb to her passing
Simple guilt of feeling nothing
She died yesterday
A heart problem

Break in Case of Emergency

They meant everything to each other
    and nothing
    even more
A perfect match
    clinging frenzied
    in no way attached
Kissing passionately
    through gritted teeth
    stained by stagnancy
Sleepless nights
    full of sweaty sex
    and sandpaper resentment
Plans were laid
    of a future
    fantasy from inception
Change was made
    in the name of hope
    but only for shallow gain
Their language
    written by friction
    was arguments and amends
"I love you" was urgent
    But words behind glass
    "Break in case of emergency"

Excitement is strong glue
      when paired with fear
      of solitude

Tough Guys Don't Cry

Chafed eyes squinting
in feigned rage against the sun
Unflinching light and his pride
combine to close off his world
Unfurled completely
in such an unexpected moment
A torrent of despair
Her hair glinting as she turned
and he learned that she
would be his no more

Sickeningly Cliché

Sickeningly cliché
The way their eyes met
Through cigarette smoke
And the lonely on parade

Guilt came straight away
Her fiancé's regret
And sure upset imagined
Saved her life this day

For to this stranger she was prey
A tasty morsel of sweat
To wet his grisly desire
Nothing left but to decay

Unspoken they parted ways
And played no duet
A threat nulled by her guilt
His gratification delayed

Stay

Sometimes, things just don't stay
No matter how much you love
No matter how much you try
Sometimes it just can't be that way

Love, though, is never in vain
It will always flow to heal
Touching on moments here and there
Always willing to replace the pain

"Just let go," they say
But this love is unbreakable
For it began before the womb
The heart must have its way

Sometimes things just don't stay

She Was Fearless

She was fearless,
For she held the silky hand of death.
Comfortable in his neutrality.
Amorous for his lusty gaze.
Seduced by his bold finality.

She was fearless,
For she knew loss was impossible.
What could you take from her?
From one who walks calm with death?
From one embracing the ultimate fear?

She was fearless,
For she could invoke him at any moment.
His sweet breath always on her neck.
A terrible blessing within her control.
In comparison, nothing is a threat.

She was fearless,
But yesterday she gave him a kiss.

Love Poem #7 - Marriage

Beauty and beast,
claiming to crave each other.
Drivel, like saliva
trickling in tempo.
Dripping convulsively
onto a floor
stained by vodka tears.
What dragon must he slay
to gain her indifference?
To bend down onto
one blood-clotted knee?
Spit still spilling
from somehow above.
Blessed they are now
by the one they detest,
in every moment but this.
So now,
it's dribble stained bliss sheets.
Convenient proximity.
Toxic normality.
Scraping dried saliva,
until they taint each other
no more.

Cloud

A cloud,
previously concealing her
now revealing her as she bleeds.
The cloud, a mystery.
Is it from she, or of she?
Engulfing
and undeniably
a force he is forced to concede.
Orange with purple sheen.
Easily seen
by others, at least.
But for which he pines incessantly!
Though, blinded, he cannot agree to
offer himself fully,
heartily and lustfully;
or to bow to any degree.
And so, she completely foresees
his demise.
For his eyes have immunity
to the powerful rhapsody
in her cloud.
Which she offers so wholly
and gracefully.

His mind fearfully searches
for her teeth.
Assuming what is kind can't be free.
So she cries, as does he,
over what, now, cannot be.
And the cloud, regretfully
retreats.

Windshield

(a micro story)

The snow melted the instant it landed on her windshield. The car heater was on maximum, keeping her warm as she sat there, outside his house. She had only planned to be there for a moment, to express how she felt and leave for good. But here she sat, twenty minutes later. She knew he was home. His car was in the driveway covered in snow. He probably hadn't left all day. His kitchen and bedroom lights were both on. She wondered if he was missing her. It hadn't been long … just a few days ago she was there with him. Her scent may still be on his pillows. She turned off the ignition and opened the car door, but then hesitated. Defeated, she slumped back into her seat and started the engine again. The cold had quickly seeped back into the car. A disappointed sigh escaped her as she thought about how good things had seemed. How right it all felt. But then he'd started to talk about her being clingy. How he wished she were more independent. How she lacked confidence. How he wanted a partner, not someone he had to look after. Why couldn't she bring herself to walk into his house and show him how strong she really was? She had the right to express her feelings too … right? These thoughts melted as they touched the windshield, on the opposite side from the falling snow. She put her pistol back in her bag and drove away.

Breadbox
(Aka. Doubtful Love)
(Aka. Temptation)

Bread goes in the breadbox
You know this
It's all you've known

And don't forget your shovel
The old one
With the shaft your hand molds to

Keep your spot in line
Protect it
You chose it after all

Remember, lightning is a snack
But it's hot
You must blow before you swallow

Now, put your eyes inside your bag
Zip it tight
It's a long walk through town

And be careful with your mind
Grip it hard
Right between madness and tedium

Loving

That Other Part of You

Lurking so deliciously
There in the shadows cast
By your sweetness
Your kindness
Your glow

Doubting my desire
To know your fullness
Your mystery
Your power
Your growl

Hints in your art
A tableau for the moment
The tears
The eyes
The tone

Bestow your presence on me fully
I'll channel the dark that flows

Prism

She is a prism
Twirl her
Dance with her
Witness her
A kaleidoscope
The refraction
The reflection
Light embraced
Light shattered
Light released
Releasing wonder
Releasing grace
Complacency
Has no place
In the spirit
Of her man

Her Love

It is green
That's all I know for sure
A deep, intoxicating shade
The rest, a mystery
Unexpectedly it consumes me
Reassuring in its warmth
Undefinable in its shape
Engulfing my life lustfully
Reverberating a glassy glee
Rearranging my essence
Reformatting my thoughts
Now I've fallen helplessly
Into the visible unseen
I do not understand
And cannot contain its power
But I know
Her love is green

A Perfect Morning

Comedian birds performing
In the ravine out the window.
Her hair resting lightly,
Highlighted by sunrise,
On my arm
And on her neck.
Sleepily she says,
"The Tom Green of birds."
And I smile.

Messes

Someone saved someone in this mess
Neither knew which
Neither cared
Two broken roads of hurt
Two shattered mirrors still shining
Two wounds in need of salve
Neither knew which
Neither cared
Someone saved someone in this mess

Her

if the sun touched her
came down from its heights
to caress her
in that meadow
where they lay breathing softly
it would abandon its power
and simply lie beside her
in awe
as he did then

Unexpected Affection

Sitting soft
Warm in your open palm
Like a sunbeam

Light exposing
Each crease, each deep scar
Bathing them in comfort

Fingers grip
Instantly it retreats
Open them again

Each muscle
Melting to relaxation
Beneath its touch

Yet quietly
It burns, caustically
Apply sunscreen

Absorb, reflect
Simply, purely accept
Its weightless gift

Sitting soft
Warm in your open palm
Like a sunbeam

Leaning

They didn't know I was watching.
Wondering how many decades they'd seen,
How many grandchildren they had,
If they met in spring.

Arm in arm, leaning into each other
They slowly entered the cafe.
How many thousands of times and
Into how many shops had they done the same?

As they leaned she asked him,
"Am I holding you up? Or are you holding me?"
And his eternally perfect answer:
"I think both, my beauty."

What Word

Does such a word exist?
A sound symbol to capture this sensation
which she so gracefully imbues.

What word combines peace with challenge,
truth with mystery, and harmony with silence?
In what phrase does one capture contentment
and mix it fully with longing?
Exhilaration and rest mix in my chest
but in no expression I have discovered.

It is likely as she explained it to me.
Some sensations are beyond the limits of language
and deserve to stay that way.

Why Do You Love Me?

Love needs no answer
to "Why?"
That would be to ask,
"Why is the sky there?"
or, "the wind blow?"
These you see and feel.
Understanding irrelevant
to their presence,
to their effect.
Like them,
love bows to no reason,
needs no justification,
requires no explanation.
Love is beyond these.
It only asks,
for acceptance.

Release

A purple cloud,
rolling electric
through soul, flesh, and neuron.
Unseeable ... but
impossible not to see.
It is Beast and Salvation.
It is Violence and Love.
An essence connected to stars
and also to veins.
Complete in knowledge
while void of logic.
Releasing a power,
unstoppable.
Throbbing slowly
into a love.
A purple cloud.

Final Note

Love, a word frivolously thrown about and ascribed to concepts that are specs of nothing. Love's true nature is the power to create and to destroy; to provide ecstasy and agony. It is agape, philia, eros, philautia, and more. Never to be understood, but forever to be craved.

The End

Jealousy and Other Terms of Endearment